Here's wl
Wl

Julie loves God and loves His Word! Having served together many years in an international Bible study, I can attest to her excellence in preparation to teach: she diligently studies the Scripture and wholeheartedly listens to God. Julie is winsome in her teaching and will engage all who participate. I look forward to many more Bible studies from her in the years to come and I know you will too. Enjoy her first "published" Bible study.

Sonya Tignor – Bible Study Teaching Leader

I have had the joy of serving with Julie in women's ministry and the pleasure of sitting under her teaching. She has the ability to share biblical truths in a way that relates to our everyday lives. She is truly a gifted teacher with a heart and passion to help women get into God's Word.

Robbie Roberts – Executive Director of Experiences and Women's Ministry Crossroads Church, Newnan, GA

You will be thoroughly blessed by this wonderful Bible study on the promises of God. Julie McCoy is passionate about the Word of God and leading people to have a growing relationship with Jesus. In this book, you'll find solid Bible teaching and real-life application. Julie will carefully guide you in a study of the Bible by drawing parallels between God's promises and Bible characters whose experience of those promises are recorded for us in the Scripture. You can enjoy this book as a personal devotional guide or as a small group study with your friends.

Dr. Tim Riordan – Pastor

SonRise Baptist Church, Newnan, GA

"*When God Promises* is a faithful, biblical call to answer life's struggles with the truth that a promise from God can be trusted. Julie has crafted for us a very practical journey from 'yeah, but' to 'even though.' Her challenge is clear and anchored in the Scriptures. The study questions provoke a personal grappling with what we really are believing when we worry and get stressed out when life isn't 'going our way.' I recommend Julie's study as a great resource for a small group or Sunday School class to stretch faith and grow trust in our Great God, El Shaddai, for whom nothing is impossible.

Mark Massey – Executive Director

Victory Family Ministries

Julie McCoy

When God
Promises

TAKING GOD AT HIS WORD WILL FREE YOU FROM
WORRY, STRESS, AND FEAR

GreenTree Publishers
Newnan, Georgia

When God Promises: Taking God at His Word will Free You from Worry, Stress, and Fear

Unless otherwise noted, Scripture taken from the Holy Bible, New International Version®, NIV®. Copyright © 1973, 1978, 1984, 2011 by Biblica, Inc.™ Used by permission of Zondervan. All rights reserved worldwide. www.zondervan.com The "NIV" and "New International Version" are trademarks registered in the United States Patent and Trademark Office by Biblica, Inc.™

Printed in the United States of America
ISBN-13: 978-1-944483-17-3 (Greentree Publishers)

Greentree Publishers
www.greentreepublishers.com

This book is dedicated to Carolyn Enis,
the teacher who introduced me to the power of
applying God's Word to my life,
who is a model of godliness,
and who never ceases to inspire me.

"Let us hold unswervingly to the hope we profess, for He who promised is faithful."
Hebrews 10:23

CONTENTS

HOW TO USE THIS STUDY

This study is designed for use by individuals or small groups. Each chapter focuses on a person in the Bible and looks at how a specific promise of God is fulfilled in his life.

The text at the beginning of the chapter follows a particular passage of Scripture giving additional insight through commentary and personal application. For individual use, begin the study by reading this section and the listed passages of Scripture. In a small group, the leader may assign this reading before the group meets, or he or she may read it as a teaching time at the beginning of the meeting.

The application questions that follow are meant to guide each participant into specific applications of the lesson. If you are doing this study individually, you may want to focus on one or two of the questions each day giving yourself time to meditate on each one. In a group study, these questions may be used as homework to be completed on the days between meetings then discussed after the teaching time. Or you may simply utilize the questions to guide discussion after the teaching.

Each week you will consider one question that asks you to list the attributes of God seen in that lesson. These are words or phrases that describe God's qualities and characteristics. Learning to identify God's attributes as you read the Bible is essential to discovering more about God Himself. In addition, compiling a list of His attributes creates a valuable resource serving as a useful reminder of who God is that will deepen your worship, your gratitude, and your confidence in His power and strength.

Following the application questions, you will find a section called "Going Deeper." This section includes questions and Scripture references that will take you deeper into a particular topic from the week's lesson. In individual study, focus on these passages of Scripture after you have completed your discussion questions. For the small group, you may want to use the "Going Deeper" questions as homework, especially if you opt not to assign the discussion questions. You may take a few minutes to discuss what the group members learned from this part of their study at the beginning of your meeting before starting on the next lesson, or they may be for personal use only.

Begin each time with prayer. Ask God to lay upon your heart the lessons He has for you and to guide you in applying them to your life. Pray for an awareness of God's leading as you read, meditate on the passages, answer the questions, and experience the transforming power of applying His Word. Ask Him to help you remain teachable and willing to be changed by the work of His Holy Spirit and thank Him in advance for the work He is going to do!

My prayer is that everyone who does this study will experience the power of God in their lives on a new level and rest in His faithfulness, trusting completely that He will do what He says He will do.

If you are not a follower of Jesus Christ, I pray that you will accept the gift of salvation He is offering you. Please read the next few pages to learn how to be saved through a personal relationship with Jesus Christ. It is only through this relationship with Jesus that we are reconciled to God and may experience His blessings.

ARE YOU SAVED?

The gospel of Jesus Christ is Good News! It is in response to the bad news that sin keeps us from having a relationship with God. Everyone sins each time we insist on doing things our way instead of God's way. Just as there are penalties for breaking a civil law, there is a penalty for sin: it is death. This death involves a total separation from God.

But here is the Good News: God loves us so much He sent His Son, Jesus Christ, to pay that penalty for us Himself. When He died on the cross, Jesus paid the penalty that you and I deserve to pay because of our sins. Imagine being found guilty in a court of law then having the judge offer to serve the time for you. That is what Jesus did for you and me. Why? Because God does not want us to suffer separation from Him. He loves us and desires a relationship with us. He knows people have a sin problem, and He provides the solution for it.

By paying the penalty for us, Jesus provides a way for our sins to be forgiven. When our sins

are forgiven, our relationship with God is restored.

Salvation can be defined as being saved from
the death and separation from God we deserve
because of our sin. Salvation is a gift that cannot
be earned. Good works cannot save you. You and
I can never be "good enough" to get to heaven
on our own no matter how hard we try. It is only
through the work Jesus did for us that we can
have eternal life. He died on the cross to pay for
our sins, and three days later He rose again to life
in victory over death. He is alive today, and
because of Him we too can experience victory
over sin and death.

Will you accept Jesus' gift of salvation today?
Your eternal life with Him begins the moment
you do. Confess to Him that you are a sinner and
that you recognize you need His salvation. Ask
Him to forgive your sins and restore your relationship with God. Turn your life over to Him
asking Him to be your Lord and your Savior.
When you do, you will be a new person! The
Holy Spirit will begin to do His work in you, and
you will reap the blessings of a child of God.

Share this exciting decision with someone you know. Seek a church home if you do not already have one and be sure you read and study the Bible as you grow in your faith.

HELPFUL SCRIPTURES

Romans 3:23 For all have sinned and fall short of the glory of God.

Romans 6:23 For the wages of sin is death, but the gift of God is eternal life in Christ Jesus our Lord.

Romans 5:8 God demonstrates his own love for us in this: While we were still sinners, Christ died for us.

Romans 10:9 If you declare with your mouth, "Jesus is Lord," and believe in your heart that God raised him from the dead, you will be saved.

John 3:16 For God so loved the world that he gave his one and only Son, that whoever believes in him shall not perish but have eternal life.

Ephesians 2:8-9 For it is by grace you have been saved, through faith—and this is not from your-selves, it is the gift of God—not by works, so that no one can boast.

CHAPTER ONE

Introduction

From "Yeah, but" to "Even though"

Howard Hendricks, a professor at Dallas Theological Seminary, once asked, "Has it occurred to you that when God shaped His message in His Book…He did it with the conscious intention of speaking directly to you, on this very day?"

Mind boggling, isn't it, to think that the God of the universe, Jehovah, God Almighty, the Great I AM was thinking of you and me and how we would benefit from reading His Word even as He was inspiring its writing? The Bible is God-breathed (2 Timothy 3:16), without error, and without contradiction. If something seems contradictory in the Scriptures you can be certain it is an issue of translation or interpretation because God will not contradict Himself. The Bible is God's message to His people; it is personal and relevant for our lives.

In this study, we will look at some specific promises God makes in His Word, how people in the Bible learned to lean on these promises, and the difference these promises made in their lives. We will see some instances where people failed to trust in God's promises and learn from them as well.

When we read the Bible, we get *information*. When we apply what we have read to our lives, we experience *transformation*. It is only in the *application* that we experience the transforming power of the Word of God. We can know what God says and even believe it, but it takes a further step to put our trust in His promises and live our lives according to His Word.

One day, I was driving home from visiting my parents, and as I drove I listened to old hymns on the radio, singing along at the top of my lungs and enjoying the fact that no one else was around to tell me to be quiet. One of my favorites, "It Is Well With My Soul" came on; I love that song! I was singing, "It is well, it is well, with my soul," believing it and meaning it with heart-felt praises coming from my lips. Suddenly, as I approached downtown Atlanta, I rounded a curve and found myself in the thick of a traffic jam. Not slow traffic. Stopped traffic. Little did I know there were three big events that evening in Atlanta. My first response was, "Oh no! I don't have time for this!" and I started fuming. Suddenly it hit me—what happened to "It is well with my soul?" I believed those words when I was singing them, didn't I? Why did it only take one snag in my day for me to gripe and complain and make it known that this situation was NOT well with my soul?

Often, we *know* God's promises, and we *believe* God's promises, but when it comes right down to it, we think our difficult circumstance is the one exception to the promise. When we are facing something that we feel is impossible, we go to God and say, "I know You said You can handle this, but there is no way. Not this time. This one is the one that is going to trip You up. Throughout the history of mankind, You have been powerful and faithful enough to keep Your promises, but this hardship I am facing is the one that is going to be too difficult for You." Of course, we don't express our feelings in those words, but when we doubt God's faithfulness and His ability to do what He promises to do, isn't that really what we are saying to Him? I call this attitude having a case of the "yeah, buts." That is when we say "**Yeah**, I know You said that You would do this, **but** I don't think You will do it this time."

God tells me I can cast my cares on Him and He will sustain me. (1 Peter 5:7)

Yeah, but I am taking care of my aging parent who has dementia and I am physically and emotionally exhausted.

God tells me to not be anxious about anything. (Philippians 4:6)

Yeah, but my husband still does not have a job and the bills are piling up.

God promises me that when I present my requests to Him with thanksgiving He will give me peace that defies all logical thinking. (Philippians 4:6-7)

Yeah, but I have a loved one who is sick or hurting and I lie awake at night worrying about them.

God promises that He will work all things for the good of those who love Him. (Romans 8:28)

Yeah, but my child is making poor choices and has gotten into trouble. I don't see how anything good can come from this situation.

> *When we get a case of the "Yeah, buts," we forget that God's promises are not dependent on circumstances in our lives being perfect.*

God tells me to forgive and that He can make my love for another increase and overflow. (Colossians 3:13 and 1 Thessalonians 3:12)

Yeah, but they have really hurt me.

You get the idea.

We have to choose to trust in the promises God has made to us. Therefore, in this study, we are going to learn to change our "yeah, but" to "even though."

Let's look at the examples from above with that simple change:

God tells me I can cast my cares on Him, and He will sustain me **even though** I am taking care of my aging parent who has dementia, and I am physically and emotionally exhausted.

God tells me to not be anxious about anything **even though** my husband still does not have a job and the bills are piling up.

God promises that when I present my requests to Him with thanksgiving, He will give me peace that defies all logical thinking **even though** I have a loved one who is sick or hurting.

God promises that He will work all things for the good of those who love Him **even though** my child is making poor choices and has gotten into trouble and I don't see how anything good can come from that.

God tells me to forgive and that He can make my love for another increase and overflow **even though** they have really hurt me.

What a difference that change in your outlook makes! Now, as we read the stories about people learning to take God at His word, let's prepare to make that change in our attitudes. Let's commit to changing our "yeah, but" to "even though." We will experience the transforming power of God's Word in our lives when we do.

APPLICATION QUESTIONS

1. When you read the Bible, do you expect to hear from God?

   How does it make you feel to know that God has a personal message for you in His Word?

2. Can you name some of the things God has promised His children?

   Which of these promises do you most need to trust right now?

3. In what circumstances are you most likely to have a "Yeah, but" attitude?

4. What do you want God to do for you through this study?

Thought for prayer this week:
It is only as we apply God's Word to our lives that we experience its transforming power.

Ask God to help you read the Bible as a personal message from Him to you, and to show you how it applies to your life.

GOING DEEPER

What promises do you see in these passages? How can you apply them to situations in your life right now?

Psalm 32:8

Psalm 91:15

Isaiah 41:10

Isaiah 48:17

Jeremiah 29:11-13

Romans 8:28

Luke 18:27

Philippians 4:19

Look back over these promises and see where in your life you are saying "Yeah, but." Now pray them back to God saying, "Even though" instead.

CHAPTER TWO:

God's Promise is Trustworthy

Genesis 12: Abraham
When God says, "I will."

When I was working as a flight attendant, I was trained to evacuate an airplane quickly in the event of an emergency. We practiced shouting the commands, "Get up! Get out! Come this way!" We needed to convey the message that now was not a time to procrastinate. Time was of the essence. Obeying the commands and leaving the airplane quickly was in the best interest of each passenger.

This tone is the same tone of the command God gave to Abram in Genesis 12:1:

The Lord had said to Abram* Go from your country, your people and your father's household to the land I will show you.

(*Abram's name was later changed to Abraham and his wife Sarai's name was changed to Sarah. Because these names are the more familiar ones, I will refer to them as Abraham and Sarah throughout this lesson)

Abraham had left his home in Ur of the Chaldeans along with his father, brothers, and their families and headed to Canaan but along the way, they stopped and settled in Haran. After his father's death God called Abraham to leave Haran.

READ GENESIS 12:1-3

There was urgency in God's command. He told Abraham to leave the security of his current way of life, leave his people, and go to a new place. Then God followed that command with the promise of great blessing in verses 2-3:

I will make you into a great nation, and I will bless you; I will make your name great, and you will be a blessing. I will bless those who bless you, and whoever curses you I will curse; and all peoples on earth will be blessed through you.

God certainly could have blessed Abraham right where he was but this promise was also a call to **obedience**. If Abraham had not obeyed God's call to go to Canaan, he would not have been where he needed to be to receive this particular blessing.

Notice in verse 1 God gave Abraham very little information about this land. Personally, I would have appreciated some photos, maybe a quick tour of the place first, at least something I could put into my GPS or check out on Google Earth. Then, I would consider whether or not that land was a place I wanted to call home. But all God told Abraham was that He would show him the land once they arrived. Abraham had to step out in faithful obedience first.

Have you ever been walking down the frozen foods aisle at the grocery store and noticed that the lights in the cases come on only as you approach each one? Each step you take causes the next case to light up. If you wait for all the lights to come on before you move forward, you won't get anywhere. Those lights illustrate how God often leads us. He gives us only what we need to get started. Once we have taken that first step of obedience, He will light the next step. On the other hand, if we choose to disobey and never step out because we want to know all of the answers first, we end up not getting anywhere at all.   Until we act on what God has given us already, He won't give us more (Mark 4: 24-25).

You may be thinking, "Of course Abraham obeyed God. He promised him some really great things;" however, trusting God may not have been that easy. Let's take a look at those promises:

God promised to make Abraham into a great nation **even though** he was childless, 75 years old, and his wife was barren (Gen 11:30).

God promised to make Abraham's name great **even though** he had no heir to carry on his name.

God promised to make Abraham a blessing so aligned with God that when someone blessed or cursed him it was as if they were blessing or cursing God Himself **even though** Abraham was just an ordinary man.

God promised that all the earth would be blessed through Abraham **even though** he was only one person.

Abraham therefore had to step out not having answers to questions like WHERE? or HOW? or WHY? It would seem that the things God promised him were impossible. He could not have a "yeah, but" attitude if he was going to be obedient to God. Go back and read those promises again replacing the phrase "even though" with "yeah, but." Do you see what a difference that makes? It brings in doubt instead of confidence and implies a need to know all the answers before moving in obedience. Abraham did not have answers, but he had **faith.**

A life of faith involves believing God and acting upon that belief.

Believing is not enough. The Bible tells us even the demons believe (James 2: 19). True faith takes God at His word and acts in obedience. Obedience then leads to blessing.

Worldly thinking tells us that we should obey only when we can be certain circumstances will fall into place according to what we want and that we should trust in the promises only after we have received the blessings. However, Scripture teaches us:

Proverbs 16:20 Whoever gives heed to instruction prospers, and blessed is the one who trusts in the Lord.

Psalm 128:1 Blessed are all who fear the Lord, who walk in obedience to Him.

Our Lives Should Follow This Pattern

TRUST → OBEDIENCE → BLESSINGS

Hebrews 11:8 states: *By faith Abraham, when called to go to a place he would later receive as his inheritance, obeyed and went, even though he did not know where he was going.*

(Did you catch the phrase "even though" in that verse?)

READ GENESIS 12:4-9

Abraham left, just as the Lord had commanded him. He left in obedience, without answers, but with a promise. Notice in verse 6 that when he and his family arrived, the Canaanites were living in the land. God had not cleared the land of its inhabitants so Abraham could waltz right in. In fact, according to Numbers 13, the cities were fortified, and the people there were giants!

In verse 7 God encouraged Abraham with a fresh revelation: He would give this land to Abraham's offspring. Offspring? Remember, Abraham is 75 years old, his wife is barren, and the land is already inhabited. But God said, "I will" and Abraham took Him at His word. In verse 7 Abraham built an altar to worship God even though the promise had not yet been fulfilled. He praised God for the promise itself. When God says He will do something, you can take Him at His word even when the circumstances you are facing make the fulfilling of His promises appear impossible.

How do you react when facing a situation that seems hopeless? Do you recall the promises of God and find peace in them? Or do you become discouraged because you don't have all the answers, thinking that God's promises can't possibly apply this time?

We can learn from Abraham's example how to take God at His word. No matter what. We have the perspective of looking through history so we know how God faithfully kept the promises He made to Abraham.

> God's faithfulness to His promises does not depend on our circumstances.

He and Sarah did indeed have a son, Isaac, and through this offspring the Hebrew people grew into a great nation. They came to possess the land God promised to Abraham. Jesus Christ's human lineage is traced back to Abraham, fulfilling God's promise to bless all people on Earth through him. God kept His promises to Abraham even though they sounded impossible at the time; He is faithful to keep His promises to us as well.

Abraham moved to the place where God led him and there built an altar to God which served as a place of worship as well as a testimony to his neighbors. He was living in God's will so everything should have been easy for him, right? Not necessarily.

READ GENESIS 12:10-13

As we read verse 10, we find that even as Abraham was living in obedience to God he faced a test of his faith in the way of a famine.

Note

Temptation vs Testing

Tests are not the same as temptations. Temptations are from Satan, who uses them to try to weaken your relationship with God. However, tests are from God, who uses them to strengthen your relationship with Him. Don't think of a test of your faith as a pass or fail situation. God is not trying to see how well you score. Instead, He is giving you the opportunity to see how trustworthy He is.

Imagine you are going skydiving. As you are getting your equipment set up, the instructor has you choose a parachute. He shows you one and says, "This one is the newest one we have. No one has ever used this kind before so I can't say if it works, but it is really pretty." Then he shows you another one and says, "This is the one I use. It always opens and has never failed me." Which one would you choose, the one that has never been tested or the one that has shown itself trustworthy time after time? Of course, you want the one that has been tested and proven!

When God allows tests in your life, He is giving you the opportunity to trust in Him and find Him faithful. The more you trust Him, the more natural it becomes to depend on Him. With that dependence comes freedom from worry and fear, because you know He will not fail you. What a beautiful result of a time of testing.

Bible scholars disagree on whether Abraham went to Egypt during the famine at God's direction or if he went there as an act of disobedience. Regardless of what influenced his decision to go, verses 11-13 show how he allowed his circumstances to change his "even though" attitude to one of "yeah, but."

Between verses 9 and 10 a change occurs in Abraham's attitude. He had stepped out in faith and trusted God's promises even though he did not have all the answers and could not yet see how the promises would be fulfilled. Yet as he headed to Egypt because of the famine, he was afraid. He was basically saying, "Yeah, I trusted You before, God, but now I have to go to Egypt and I will be in danger there. Yeah, I know You have made great promises to me, but I am afraid because they may kill me in order to get to Sarah."

This was a legitimate fear. In that culture, at that time, a man could be killed if someone powerful wanted his wife. Instead of trusting that God would protect him, Abraham concocted a scheme. A woman's brother would be responsible for arranging her marriage, so if Sarah claimed that Abraham was her brother instead of her husband, he would be safe. Think about it. If Abraham had been killed in Egypt his death would have prevented God from giving him an heir, making him a great nation or any of the other things He had promised. If Abraham had fully trusted God to keep His promises, he would have known that God would protect him in Egypt.

Instead he panicked and trusted in a lie for protection of his life. In this passage, his faith became scheming, his confidence became fear, and his focus turned from God to people.

READ GENESIS 12:14-16

At first, Abraham's plan seemed to be a success. Pharaoh did, indeed, want Sarah to be one of his wives, and Abraham was treated with respect because they thought he was Sarah's brother. But that is not the end of the story.

READ GENESIS 12:17-20

When a woman was taken into the household of Pharaoh, a long time of preparation ensued before she was actually presented to him. In God's sovereignty, He exposed Abraham's lie before any harm could come to Sarah. God's protection is evident in these verses as Pharaoh gave Sarah back to Abraham and sent them away, giving his men orders that would provide physical protection for Abraham and Sarah as they left. In His mercy and grace, God rescued them.

Abraham was to be a source of blessing, but in his disobedience, he was a cause of judgment, not only on himself, but on the entire household of Pharaoh. Abraham appears to be rewarded in his deception because verse 16 says he acquired wealth from Pharaoh. However, the story continues in chapter 13 and the large herds of livestock he was given created a rift between Abraham and

Lot, causing them to part ways. In addition, Hagar, Sarah's Egyptian maidservant, was most likely acquired during this time and she, along with her son, Ishmael, were the cause of much grief for Abraham and Sarah. (You can read their story in Genesis 16).

Abraham's failure to trust God in this situation caused him to face consequences but when he repented and turned back to God (Genesis 13:4) he was forgiven and his relationship with God was restored. We all have a tendency to sin and falter in our

> God's purposes will be accomplished even when we interfere, but there will still be consequences to face for our disobedience.

walk with the Lord, even as we are growing in our faith. The work of the Holy Spirit in our lives is a life-long process called sanctification. This is not an instant transformation where we suddenly become perfect but rather it is a process through which we make progress in becoming more like Christ. When we sin like Abraham and turn from faith to schemes because of our "yeah, but" attitude, we need to recognize it, confess it, and turn back to God.

If you have a relationship with God through Jesus Christ, no failure is permanent. He promises to forgive our sins and restore our relationship with Him.

You can know that when God says, "I will….," He is faithful to do it.

APPLICATION QUESTIONS

1. What reasons could Abraham have had for not trusting God's promises?
    (What do Hebrews 11:8 and 11:11 say about this?)

    What do you think would have happened if Abraham had decided not to obey God's call?

2. Compare Abraham's responses in Gen 12:4 and 12:7 with how he responded in Gen. 12:11-13. What do you think made the difference?

3. Would it have been easier for Abraham to trust God's promises if Isaac had already been born or if the Promised Land was ready for him to inhabit?

Why do you think God waited to fulfill those promises?

4. Where are you holding back on trusting God because you think something is impossible since you can't see how God can work it out?

    Do you feel like you need to have all the answers before you step out in obedience to God?

    How can you change your "yeah, but" attitude to "even though?"

5. What attributes of God do you see in this passage?

Thought for prayer this week:
A life of faith relies on God's Word
instead of man's schemes.

In what areas are you scheming to manipulate circumstances instead of trusting God to work through them? Ask God to show you specifically where you need to work on this.

GOING DEEPER

Look at these verses and write what these promises mean to you.

Deuteronomy 31:8

Joshua 1:5

Psalm 32:8

Isaiah 41:10

Matthew 11:28

2 Corinthians 6:16

Hebrews 10:23

Using your Bible's concordance or a Bible search, look up verses about FEAR (not God-fearing but about being afraid).

Choose one or two and write down what they say
about fear.

Can you find any verses where God tells us He
wants us to be afraid?

CHAPTER THREE

God's Presence is Powerful

Genesis 39-41: Joseph
When God says, "I am with you"

A few years ago, my daughter broke her leg while warming up at a horse show. As soon as she fell, someone came to get me so I could be with her. I rode with her in the ambulance and stayed with her in the emergency room. Her dad and brother came to the hospital so they could be with her as well. But as they wheeled her to the operating room we came to a point where we could no longer stay with her. They took her one way while we were directed to a waiting room in the opposite direction. As her mom, that separation was probably more difficult for me than it was for her. I knew there was nothing I could do for her physically; nonetheless I wanted to stay with her. I was comforted by realizing that God Himself could go places I could not and that He would be with her during the surgery even as He was with me in the waiting room.

When God says, "I am with you" what do those words really mean to us? Do they mean we will be protected from disappointment or hurt? How can we know God is with us if we can't see Him? What about times when we are facing very difficult situations—is God with us then?

Let's look at the life of Joseph and what Scripture means when it says, "God was with him."

Joseph, a descendant of Abraham, was born to Jacob and his wife Rachel. Jacob had twelve sons, by wives and maidservants. Rachel was Jacob's one true love and the two sons she bore, Joseph and Benjamin, were clearly Jacob's favorites.

Joseph's brothers resented his position as a favored son (Gen 37:4). When Joseph had two dreams that foretold his brothers bowing down to him and he shared these dreams with his brothers, their jealousy and ill feelings toward him increased. His brothers sold Joseph into slavery and told Jacob he was dead. Joseph was taken to Egypt as a slave in Potiphar's house, which is where this lesson begins.

READ GENESIS 39:1-6

We see that:

verse 2 The Lord was with Joseph and he prospered.

verse 3 His master saw that the Lord was with him.

verse 3 The Lord gave him success in everything he did.

verse 5 The Lord blessed the household because of Joseph.

verse 5 The blessing of the Lord was on everything Potiphar had.

Success? Prospering? Joseph was a slave. He had been betrayed by his brothers, sold into slavery and taken from his homeland to Egypt, yet Scripture says the Lord gave him success in everything he did. Wouldn't success have meant he was freed and allowed to go back home?

> *Success does not mean God changes our circumstances but that He blesses us in those circumstances.*

Frustration comes when we define success as getting what we want rather than seeing it as God achieving His purpose in our life.

God was doing a mighty work in Joseph's life even during his time in slavery. He was preparing Joseph for a position of great influence and authority although Joseph had no way of knowing that. What he did know was that God was with him. Rather than having an attitude of "Yeah, God says He is with me, but how can that be if these bad things are happening?" he looked at his circumstances with the attitude of "Even though these things are happening, I know God is with me." This attitude had an impact on those around him. In verse 3, Potiphar recognized that it was the Lord who gave Joseph his success.

At this point in the story, Joseph was success-ful: witnessing God's presence and power in his life, in a position of authority in Potiphar's house, and fulfilling his duties so well Potiphar did not have to concern himself with anything except what he was going to eat. When Potiphar's wife tried to coax Joseph into bed with her, he refused, calling it a sin against God. Day after day she tried, and day after day he resisted (verses 6-

10). Joseph responded with integrity out of loyalty to Potiphar and to God.

READ GENESIS 39:11-23

Falsely accused. Thrown into prison. Had God now forsaken Joseph? Not at all! The Lord was with Joseph and continued to give Joseph success in everything he did. In light of our new definition of success as "God's purposes being achieved in our lives," we can now see that Joseph was indeed successful.

In fact, when we look more closely at Joseph's circumstances, God's hand is seen in every detail.

> *Our suffering is not an indication of God's absence.*

Potiphar could have had Joseph executed, but God restrained Potiphar's anger and protected Joseph. Joseph was put in the prison with the king's prisoners, a situation that would put him in contact with the man who would ultimately be instrumental in Joseph's release. God was still training Joseph and his time in prison gave him the opportunity to learn to wait on God's timing.

Joseph did what was right, yet still found himself facing difficulties. Joseph's suffering was not because God left him but because God was working on him. God tells us that times of suffering have purpose.

Consider Romans 5:3-5:

Not only so, but we also glory in our sufferings, because we know that suffering produces perseverance; perseverance, character; and character, hope. And hope does not put us to shame, because God's love has been poured out into our hearts through the Holy Spirit, who has been given to us.

And James 1:2-4:

Consider it pure joy, my brothers and sisters, whenever you face trials of many kinds because you know that the testing of your faith produces perseverance. Let perseverance finish its work so that you may be mature and complete, not lacking anything.

Look at what God promises when we persevere in suffering: character, hope, confidence in God's love, joy, maturity, completion, and provision.

We all suffer at one time or another. If you have not faced a trial lately, just hang on, because you will eventually. When we consider all that

God can do in us during these times, we can be assured of His presence, rather than feeling like He has left us. Everyone faces times of suffering; be careful not to waste yours. Remain teachable and experience the growth that comes with perseverance. Ask God to help you see trials as times of teaching, not of tragedy.

The story continues with Joseph once again put in charge, but this time in the prison. The Lord continued to be with him and gave him success in whatever he did.

READ GENESIS 40:1-7

Joseph's circumstances included being hated and betrayed by his brothers, sold into slavery, harassed by his master's wife, falsely accused, and unjustly imprisoned. Yet here, rather than wallowing in self-pity, he showed concern when two prisoners under his care looked sad. Because self-pity is by definition a self-indulgent attitude, Joseph would never have noticed his fellow prisoners' sadness had he been feeling sorry for himself.

Have you ever planned a big party? For weeks, maybe months, your thoughts are consumed by the event. Even seemingly unrelated things bring your mind back to the theme, the food, the decorations, or the guest list. Everything else is pushed aside temporarily as your mind focuses on the big event.

We behave the same way when we decide to throw a big pity party with ourselves as the guest of honor. Every little thing brings to mind that injustice we suffered—the hurt, the disappointment, or the pain. All else is pushed aside, so we can fully focus on our self-pity. Falling into this trap is easy when things are not going our way.

If anyone deserved to throw himself a pity party, it was Joseph. How was he able to fight the temptation to feel sorry for himself? It was not because he loved his circumstances; it was because he knew the Lord was with him.

Why did I want to be with my daughter when she broke her leg? I wanted her to know she was not facing this tragedy alone. Because I knew her better than anyone else there, I knew what frightened her, and I knew what comforted her. I wanted to be her advocate and her support, a source of strength and encouragement as she faced something painful and difficult.

God's presence accomplishes for us all I wanted to do for my daughter and more. He is omnipresent, which means He is everywhere.

However, His being "with" Joseph refers to His special, inspiring, comforting presence, His face shining on him, and the awareness in Jo-

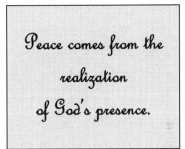

Peace comes from the realization of God's presence.

seph's heart that he was not alone.

Consider these verses:

Isaiah 41:10 So do not fear, for I am with you.

God wants the awareness of His presence to calm your fears.

Matthew 10: 29-31 Are not two sparrows sold for a penny? Yet not one of them will fall to the ground outside your Father's care. And even the very hairs of your head are all numbered. So, don't be afraid; you are worth more than many sparrows.

God knows what you are going through. In fact, He knows everything about you. Do not fall for the lie that God is too busy with the "big" things to care about what is going

on in your life. He cares about the smallest creatures, and He cares about you.

Psalm 36:7 How priceless is your unfailing love, O God! People take refuge in the shadow of your wings.

God's love for you is unfailing. That not only means it will never break down, it also means His love will never fail you. God's love for you means His plan for your life is perfect. He loves you too much for anything less.

John 16:33 I have told you these things, so that in me you may have peace. In this world, you will have trouble. But take heart! I have overcome the world.

Nothing you face is too big for God to handle. He wants you to have peace in knowing that.

Joseph faced his difficulties without complaint because of his awareness of God's presence and the power of God working in his life. God gave him the correct interpretations of the baker's and cupbearer's dreams, which eventually led to his being called to appear before Pharaoh who sought interpretation of two disturbing dreams of his own. Joseph's ability to interpret the dreams for Pharaoh ultimately brought about his release.

READ GENESIS 41:14-16

Notice Joseph's reply in verse 16: *I cannot do it, but God will give Pharaoh the answer he desires.* If ever there was a time for Joseph to try to make himself look good in Pharaoh's eyes, this was it. Instead, he humbly gave God all the credit, and as he explained to Pharaoh the meaning of the dreams in verses 25-32, Joseph continued to give God all the glory (verses 25, 28, 32). Joseph explained that God was revealing in the dreams seven years of abundance followed by seven years of famine. He spelled out a plan for storing food during the times of abundance to carry them through the years of famine and Joseph made it clear that this was God's revelation, God's plan, and God's timing.

READ GENESIS 41:37-43

Look closely at verse 38. Do you see what impressed Pharaoh? Joseph was one in whom is the spirit of God. God's presence in Joseph's life was evident even to Pharaoh. Even though Joseph was a Hebrew, a slave, and a prisoner, God was with him, and it showed.

As he was being carried off by slave traders Joseph did not know God was placing him in Egypt, exactly where he needed to be to carry out God's plan. As he was a slave in Potiphar's house he did not know God was training him in administrative skills he would later use in a position of great power. As he was falsely accused and thrown into prison he did not know God was teaching him compassion and humility. Finally, as he was waiting to be released from prison he did not know God was teaching him to wait patiently on His perfect timing. As he faced these times of intense trials, Joseph kept his "even though" attitude, trusting God to keep His Word.

Thirteen years passed from the time Joseph was sold by his brothers into slavery until he was given this position of authority by Pharaoh. For those thirteen years he could have been nursing a grudge, holding onto anger at his brothers and at God, and lost in despair; instead, he allowed God to work in him even though things were not going his way. He found strength and success through God's presence in his life even though he could not understand why things were happening the way they were.

Joseph could not foresee God's plan for his life, but he knew God was with him. He held onto his trust in the faithfulness of God. He knew that even though his circumstances looked hopeless at times, God was always in control, and nothing is ever hopeless with God. This is God's promise to us as well. The same God who was with Joseph is with us. We can have peace in that knowledge even though things may not be going our way.

We experience God's presence through a relationship with Jesus Christ. If you do not know Jesus as your Lord and Savior or if you are not sure of your salvation, please go to the section at the front of this book entitled "Are You Saved?" to read how to accept His gift of salvation. Speak to someone at church, a friend, or a group leader. Do not waste another day without experiencing the power of the presence of God in your life.

APPLICATION QUESTIONS

1. How does the world define "success"?

    How is that definition different from how
    God would define it?

2. How do you think awareness of God's
    presence made a difference to Joseph in his
    life...
    ...In Potiphar's house?
    ...In prison?
    ...Going before Pharaoh?
    ...Working for Pharaoh?

3. Where in your life do you need to become
    more aware of God's presence, and what
    difference do you think that awareness will
    make?

4. How can others be blessed by the presence of God in your life?

How does complaining affect your testimony?

5. What attributes of God do you see in this passage?

6. When are you tempted to take glory for yourself instead of giving it to God?

> *Thought for prayer this week*
>
> *God's silence does not indicate His absence.*

Ask God to help you be more aware of His presence, especially in areas of your life where you are suffering or waiting.

GOING DEEPER

Look up these verses and write down how they were illustrated in Joseph's life. Then write specific situations in your life where you will put your faith in these promises.

Joshua 1:9

Psalm 1:1-3

Psalm 27:14

Isaiah 43:2

John 12:26

2 Corinthians 12:9-10

Read Psalm 105:1-22. What phrases speak of God's faithfulness?

What phrases speak of His power?

Which one means the most to you?

CHAPTER FOUR

God's Plan is Perfect

When God says, "In all things I will work for your good..."
Genesis 42-45: Joseph

"Praise God! The car just died!"

I was a college student headed home for the weekend riding with two guys who were friends of friends of mine. I had met them several times, but I did not know them well. We were listening to a tape of Christian praise music and even though I knew these guys were followers of Christ, I was still caught off guard when the driver started praising God as the engine died and the car rolled onto the shoulder of the interstate. Words of praise were not what came to my mind as I realized our situation!

This was a time before cell phones, so we did what folks did when their car broke down: we opened the hood, looked around, and waited. A kind man in a business suit stopped to offer help and ended up giving us a ride to the home of the owner of the car. As he was driving us, the young men I was with started a light-hearted conversation with him about Jesus. They began by asking if they could play the tape we had been listening to (I never would have thought to grab that tape and bring it with us). I was mesmerized as I listened to them witnessing to this man in such a loving and joyful way. When we arrived at the house and got out of the car, the man thanked them and said he was going to get things right with God and get back into church.

That is when I understood the appropriateness of praising God when the car died. Our circumstance was bad, but through it God was doing a good work, not only in that businessman's life but in mine as well.

READ ROMANS 8:28-29

Trusting in God's promise to work all things for our good can be difficult when we are in the midst of a trying time. Because of the limitations of our human minds, we can't see how something terrible could possibly be used for something good, and that mindset can lead us into a "yeah, but" attitude. We cry out to God saying, "Yeah,

God, you said you will work things for my good, but there is no way good can come from this hopeless situation!"

Not only is God not limited by our short-sightedness, but His faithfulness to His promises is not affected by our circumstances. Therefore, we can face difficulties knowing that He is working things for our good even though we don't yet see how He is going to accomplish it.

God's plan is not limited by our short-sightedness.

God worked out this promise in Joseph's life as his story continues in Genesis 42. As you recall from our last lesson Joseph's brothers had sold him into slavery and he was taken to Egypt where he worked in Potiphar's house. Because God was with him and gave him success in everything he did, Joseph went from being a slave to becoming second-in-command under Pharaoh. Joseph was directed by God to collect and store grain during the years of plenty so when the famine struck there was food in Egypt when there was not any in the rest of the world. According to Genesis 41:57 all the world came to Egypt to buy grain from Joseph because the famine was severe everywhere.

READ GENESIS 42:1-5

(Note: God changed Jacob's name to Israel in Genesis 35:10. In these verses he is referred to as both Jacob and Israel)

Joseph's family in Canaan was starving so Jacob sent ten of his sons to Egypt to buy some of the grain stored there. Since Joseph and Benjamin were Jacob's favorite sons, his fear that some harm might come to Benjamin if he sent him with his brothers may be an indication that he suspected the other brothers' responsibility in Joseph's disappearance. At this time, Jacob thought Joseph was dead because that is what his other sons had told him, so he was protective of Benjamin and still openly favored him over the others.

READ GENESIS 42:6-9

While he was a young man still living in Canaan, Joseph had two dreams in which his brothers were bowing down to him. Genesis 37:8 tells that when he told his brothers about the dreams it made them hate him all the more. However, God's promise in those dreams stayed with Joseph and undoubtedly gave him strength and hope in his times of suffering. God had a plan for Joseph's life. When his brothers bowed down to him, Joseph knew God's promise was being kept and His plan was being carried out.

He recognized his brothers but they had no idea the man they were facing was Joseph. Twenty-two years had passed since they had sold him to the slave traders and they assumed he was dead. Joseph would put them through a series of tests before he revealed his identity to them.

Joseph did not act out of revenge or vindictiveness. Never do we read in Scripture that he wept while he was enslaved or in prison, yet Joseph wept time and time again for his brothers. Human emotion would call for revenge, but the Lord was still with Joseph and gave him a desire to see them restored, not destroyed.

For twenty-two years Joseph's brothers lived with guilt over what they had done to him. God would now use Joseph as His instrument to bring about their repentance, forgiveness and restoration. Only then would they experience true peace.

Consider Hebrews 12:11:

No discipline seems pleasant at the time, but painful. Later on, however, it produces a harvest of righteousness and peace for those who have been trained by it.

Keep this in mind when you feel God is dealing harshly with you.

Joseph accused his brothers of being spies. Of course, he knew that was not true, but as they defended themselves against his accusations, their sin against Joseph was brought to the forefront of

> *The benefit of God working in you as He disciplines you far outweighs the unpleasantness of the process.*

their minds. In verse 13, they had to admit one of their brothers "is no more." As they spent three days in prison, they began to see the correlation between their sin and their current trials.

READ GENESIS 42: 21-26

Identifying their sin was the first step toward their restoration, but at this point they showed more remorse than repentance. Joseph would continue to test them to bring them to a place of true repentance.

Note

Remorse is not the same as repentance

Remorse is the feeling one has because they are guilty of something, often brought about because of getting caught and suffering consequences. Feelings of remorse can be a heavy weight on your life, and the result can be debilitating. **Repentance** involves confessing sin to God (identifying it as sin instead of trying to justify it), asking Him for forgiveness and praying for His help in changing a sinful attitude or action. This change makes all the difference and ultimately leads to freedom from guilt.

> 2 Corinthians 7:10 teaches:
>
> *Godly sorrow brings repentance that leads to salvation and leaves no regret, but worldly sorrow brings death.*

In verse 27, the brothers discovered the silver Joseph had put into their sacks, and they were terrified. In verse 28, they started to perceive God's hand in their situation but still failed to trust that what He was doing was for their good. How they must have dreaded going home and telling Jacob everything that had happened! They had to tell him they had been accused of being spies, Simeon had been imprisoned and would not be released until they returned with Benjamin, and they had discovered the payment they had taken for the grain was still in their sacks.

READ GENESIS 42:36

Jacob's reaction to their news was as they had predicted. "Everything is against me!" he wailed. This is Jacob's "yeah, but" moment. In Genesis 35:3 Jacob had declared: *Then come, let us go up to Bethel, where I will build an altar to God, who answered me in the day of my distress and who has been with me wherever I have gone.*

Jacob had experienced God's help in a time of distress and knew what it felt like to be aware of God's presence. However, instead of remembering that and trusting God in this difficult circumstance, his attitude was "Yeah, but these terrible things are happening to me right now and that can't possibly be good." He had no idea these events were actually working for his benefit. These were not good things, but God would still use them to bring about good for Jacob and his family.

> God does not promise that only good things will happen to those who love Him, but He promises that He is working for their good in all things that happen to them.

Can you relate to Jacob? How easy it is to forget what God has done for us in the past. Our natural reaction to trials, hurts, and disappointment is like Jacob's. The God who was with

Jacob in Genesis 35 was still with him in Genesis 42, and He is the same God who is with us today. When you find you are tempted to view your life's circumstances with a "yeah, but" attitude, go back to your list of God's attributes. Ask Him to help you remember all He has done for you. Be intentional about trusting God's plan for your good regardless of how you perceive the things happening to you.

READ GENESIS 43:11-14

Finally, the grain had run out, and Jacob had no choice but to send his sons back to Egypt for more. He sent them off with a prayer for their safe return.

When they arrived in Egypt, the brothers were warmly received. Simeon was released to them and they were invited to a feast at Joseph's house.

READ GENESIS 43:32-34

Joseph needed to determine the brothers' attitude toward Benjamin. Were they as hateful toward him as they had been toward Joseph? He watched their reaction as Benjamin was served five times as much as the others. This feast also served as an indication to the brothers that they had found favor in Joseph's eyes; therefore, they feasted and drank freely. They were relieved but still had not dealt with their sin.

Isaiah 32:17 says: *The fruit of that righteousness will be peace; its effect will be quietness and confidence forever.*

Righteousness is being in right standing with God which is only possible through a relationship with Jesus Christ. Only in righteousness will there be true, lasting peace; its effect will be quietness and confidence forever.

Because his brothers still needed to come to a point of repentance, Joseph had one last test for them. As they prepared to return home, their silver was once again placed in their sacks and Joseph's silver cup was hidden in Benjamin's sack as well. Joseph then sent his steward to confront them.

READ GENESIS 44:6-9

When the cup was found in Benjamin's sack, the brothers were devastated. Genesis 37:34 describes Jacob tearing his clothes in despair over

the loss of Joseph. Now, his sons tore their
clothes as Benjamin was accused. What a contrast
between that attitude toward Benjamin and how
they had felt toward Joseph! As Joseph's brothers
acknowledged their sin before God they began to
take responsibility for what they had done (verses
16 and 20). They became repentant at last. Further evidence of a change of heart is found in
Judah's plea in verses 18-33.

READ GENESIS 44:30-34

Do not miss the parallel here between Judah's
offer to pay the penalty in Benjamin's place and
the sacrifice of Jesus Christ. When Jesus, who was
from the line of Judah, died on the cross, He was
paying for our sins, taking our death penalty so
we may have life. As a foreshadowing of that
sacrifice, Judah was willing to become a servant
so Benjamin could remain free.

READ GENESIS 45:1-8

Joseph could no longer contain himself.
Realizing God had brought them to full repentance, he wept as he revealed his identity to his

brothers. Read verses 5-8 again and notice Joseph's "even though" attitude: **Even though** you hated me and sold me into slavery, God was sending me here to save lives. **Even though** I was falsely accused and thrown into prison, God was preparing me to work out His plan to preserve His people. **Even though** you had a plan that was evil, God's plan was for good (see also Genesis 50:20). Notice Joseph's forgiveness was not dependent on an apology from his brothers. He could forgive them because of his trust in God's plan and his "even though" perspective of the events that had occurred.

After twenty-two years, Joseph's brothers were brought to a place of repentance, forgiveness, and restoration. Their restoration came about not because of their gifts, their sacrifices, or even their confession, but because they were forgiven. This forgiveness was purchased on their behalf through Joseph's suffering, serving as another picture of what Jesus would do for us on the cross.

Joseph's brothers returned to Canaan to bring Jacob and the rest of the family back to Egypt.

Finally, Jacob was able to see how God had been working for his good all along.

As we read Joseph's story, we feel sadness for him in his suffering, but as he faces each difficult circumstance we cheer him on saying, "Hang on Joseph! Everything that is happening to you is all part of a great plan! There is a happy ending!" We say these words with confidence because we can read ahead and know what is going to happen. We know that Joseph was restored in ways he could never have imagined, and because of his obedience to God's will lives were saved. But that is not all. We also know that right now Joseph is with Jesus in heaven where everything was ultimately leading him. No pain, no suffering, no betrayal, slavery, or prison—forever.

When God is viewing your life, cheering you on, telling you to hang on, and promising you that He is working for your good you can trust in that because He knows how your story ends. He is at work in your circumstances shaping you and molding you to be more like Christ. He knows that because of your relationship with Jesus Christ, you have a happy ending like Joseph.

2 Corinthians 4:17 says: *For our light and momentary troubles are achieving for us an eternal glory that far outweighs them all.*

God knows the end of your story. So, when your "yeah, but" attitude has you saying, "Everything is against me!" remember God's promise to work for your good in all things. Keep in mind that when God says "All" that includes everything you are facing, without exception.

APPLICATION QUESTIONS

1. If you were in Joseph's position, what do you think your reaction would be to seeing your brothers?

    How could Joseph react the way he did?

    What good would have come if Joseph had reacted with vengeance?

2. Compare the bad things Jacob and his sons had to endure with the good things that came from them.

    What lesson does God have for you in this comparison?

3. In what situations in your life do you need to shift your focus from "yeah, but" to "even though" concerning the GOOD God is working?

4. What attributes of God do you see in this passage?

Thought for prayer this week

The more you yield your life to God, the more He will give you both spiritual and practical wisdom for every circumstance.

Ask God to show you where your reactions are flesh-controlled (yeah, but) and not spirit-controlled (even though). Turn those circumstances over to God, act according to His will, and take Him at His word when He promises to work good through every situation.

GOING DEEPER

Look up these verses and write down key words that pertain to Joseph's life and to yours.

Psalm 30:5

John 16:20-22

John 16:33

2 Corinthians 4:17

2 Corinthians 4:18

How can these promises change your attitude to help you have God's perspective on the situations in your life?

Read 2 Corinthians 3:17. What does God promise us in this verse?

Where do you need God's freedom from a grudge? Anger? Hurt feelings?

Will you confess that right now, asking God to influence your attitude?

Where is God encouraging you to take Him at His word, trusting in the promise that He is working GOOD for you in ALL your circumstances?

CHAPTER FIVE
God's Provision is Sufficient

When God says, "I AM"
Exodus 3:1-4:17: Moses

His name was John.

I was working a flight from Atlanta to Seattle and I sat down for a break after completing the meal service. A passenger approached me and commented that he liked my cross lapel pin. He then went on to say, "I would like to know about Jesus." It took a few seconds for his comment to register in my mind. I had just been given a golden opportunity to share the Gospel of Jesus Christ with someone who was seeking Him! Because it was a long flight we had plenty of time to talk. He knew Jesus had died for him but did not understand why His death was necessary. He was surprised to hear that he could be forgiven of his sins and have a relationship with Jesus just by asking for it. What a blessing it was for me to give him the Good News. I will not see John again until we meet in heaven, but because he chose to accept the gift of salvation Jesus offered him, I know he will be there.

When I woke up that morning and got ready for work, I did not have any idea what my day would entail. It was an ordinary day. I was an ordinary flight attendant going on an ordinary trip. But the God I serve is extraordinary and His hand on the events of that day changed the eternal destiny of a man named John.

This week's lesson begins with an ordinary day in Moses' life. He had given up his life in the palace as the son of Pharaoh's daughter to identify with and deliver his people, the Hebrews (also referred to as the nation of Israel or the Jews) who had been enslaved by the Egyptians for over 400 years. Exodus 2 tells how Moses started his crusade for deliverance by killing an Egyptian who was abusing a Hebrew slave. Not only was his act not appreciated by the Hebrews, but Pharaoh put a price on his head necessitating his flight from Egypt. He had settled in Midian where he married Zipporah and worked for her father as a shepherd for forty years.

READ EXODUS 3:1-5

Moses was tending his father-in-law's flock just like he had done every day for the past forty years. As a shepherd, he was constantly on the lookout for anything that could pose a threat to the sheep. As he scanned his surroundings, he spotted a bush that was on fire. Not a regal cedar tree or a shade-producing fig tree, but a thorny, ordinary, run-of-the-mill bush. Moses noticed that the flames were not consuming the bush as it burned, so he moved closer to investigate.

As Moses approached the bush, he heard God's voice from within the bush calling him by name. God certainly had his attention now. His reply was, "Here I am." Moses was then instructed to take off his sandals because he was standing on holy ground.

That day started like every other day in Moses' life for the past forty years. That bush was one of many bushes in the desert. That ground was the same ground he had walked on many times while he was out with the flocks.

An encounter with God changes everything.

So, what made the difference that day? The presence of God Almighty!

An ordinary day became extraordinary when Moses had a personal encounter with God. An ordinary bush and ordinary dirt became extra-ordinary when God's presence rested in them.

READ EXODUS 3:6

Notice that as God identified Himself to Moses He said "I am." Present tense, not past. *I am the God of your father, the God of Abraham, the God of Isaac and the God of Jacob.* He was letting Moses know that He was the same God who made the covenant with Abraham, and the same God who identified Himself to Isaac and to Jacob.

He is also that same God today. When you wrap your mind around the fact that the God you read about in the Bible is the same God who desires a personal relationship with you, doesn't that knowledge thrill you? The God who heard the cries of His people and who was so concerned about their suffering that He came down to rescue them (verses 7-8) is the God who has done the same for you and me. This is a foreshadowing, a promise, of the work of Jesus

Christ who came down from heaven to rescue His children from the bondage of sin.

As God told Moses He would deliver the Israelites from Egypt and bring them to the Promised Land, we can imagine Moses' excitement mounting. Finally, his people were going to be freed. However, God dropped the bombshell in verse 10: *So now go. I am sending you to Pharaoh to bring my people the Israelites out of Egypt* (emphasis mine). And then Moses started his list of "yeah, but" excuses.

READ EXODUS 3:11-12

Moses essentially said to God, "I am just an ordinary man! I can't do this!" Remember, Moses had left Egypt as a failure. His attempt to deliver his people through his plan in his power had led only to him having to flee with a price on his head. Have you ever felt like that? Have you experienced God calling you to do something you think is just too hard? Something you do not feel qualified to do? Do you allow the devil to discourage you by convincing you that you are a failure? In verse 12, God responds to Moses' objections by saying, "I will be with you".

God did not say to Moses, "You are the great and powerful Moses. You will be fine because you are so smart. You can do this." Because the deliverance of the Israelites was not about Moses at all. This was about what God was going to do. Moses was correct in thinking he was just an ordinary man but what he failed to recognize was that the extraordinary God who

> When God calls you to do something, He sufficiently equips you to do it.

was calling him would sufficiently equip him. Moses was not going in his own power, but God's.

Second Corinthians 9:8 says: *God is able to bless you abundantly, so that in all things at all times, having all that you need, you will abound in every good work.*

How often do you give God your "yeah, but" excuses because you think you are inadequate to do what He is calling you to do? That sense of personal inadequacy is actually necessary if you are going to be used effectively by God because it means you recognize your need for Him. Self-reliance is not a fruit of the Spirit! God wants to exhibit His power in you and through you. The verse above promises He will give you ALL that you need to do the good work He has for you.

Matthew Henry put it this way: "God's presence puts an honour upon the worthless, wisdom and strength into the weak and foolish, makes the greatest difficulties dwindle to nothing, and is enough to answer all objections."[1]

Continuing in verse 12, God promised Moses success and told him they would come back to that very mountain and worship Him (a promise fulfilled in Exodus 18). He used definite words like, "*When* you have brought the people out" and "You *will* worship God on this mountain" (emphasis mine). Yet Moses' "yeah, but" attitude was still evident.

> *God is not looking for expertise; He is looking for obedience.*

---

[1] Henry, M. (1994). *Matthew Henry's commentary on the whole Bible: complete and unabridged in one volume* (p. 99). Peabody: Hendrickson.

God promised to go with Moses, that he would successfully bring the Israelites out of Egypt and they would come back to that same place and worship Him. What was Moses' response? "Yeah, but what if they ask who sent me?"

God's reply in verse 14 was not flippant or evasive; in fact, it was incredibly powerful. God addressed Moses' objections by revealing something of His own character. When He called himself "I AM WHO I AM," He was saying that He is real, self-existent, self-sufficient, and eternal. He has no origin and answers to no one. He does not need anything from anyone. He is the God who is, who was, and who is to come (Revelation 1:8).

He was identifying Himself as the unchangeable, all-powerful, trustworthy God. That was the authority by which Moses was sent and the power by which these things would be accomplished.

Even after God's promises of success in verses 17 and 20, Moses continued to offer excuses. How often do we fall into the trap of

thinking we could be obedient to God's call if
only we knew the outcome? We convince
ourselves that it is okay to delay our obedience
until we can be sure
we will succeed.
Here, God had given
Moses that assur-
ance and he was still
hesitant. Moses' re-
sponse in chapter 4
begins with those
words that line up so

When God promises "I will be with you," that promise includes everything that He is.

nicely with our "yeah, but. They are "What if…"

God is not going to call you to do something,
promise to equip you to do it, and then fill your
mind with "what if" scenarios that cause you fear
and discouragement. The beauty of trusting the
Almighty, Sovereign God is that you never have
to concern yourself with the "what ifs!" So, if
those thoughts are crowding out your trust in
God's plan, you need to recognize they not
coming from God and be intentional about
refusing to listen to them. Whenever you are
tempted to play a "what if" scenario in your head,
replace it instead with the things you know are

true about God: He is sovereign. He is all-powerful. He has a perfect plan. He will equip you. He is with you. Continue the list with the truths about God you need to hear.

READ EXODUS 4:1-5

In this chapter God gives Moses a visible illustration of what I describe in the paragraph above. He replaced Moses' "what if" scenario with a display of His power.

My house is surrounded by woods, and I am well aware that there are snakes sharing this property with me. I recognize there are good snakes providing beneficial services such as killing poisonous snakes and rodents; however, I have decided my aversion to them is biblical (See Genesis 3). I do not like snakes and therefore I can relate to Moses' reaction in verse 3 where he ran from the snake that was produced when he threw his staff on the ground.

In verse 4, God told Moses, who had just run away from the snake, to pick it up by the tail. He did not tell Moses what would happen next; He just expected his obedience. *So, Moses reached out and took hold of the snake.* We could certainly understand if Moses had said, "**Yeah, but** it's a snake!" Instead, he took hold of it **even though** it was a snake. Only after his obedience (throwing down the staff and picking up the snake) did Moses experience the miracles.

God gave Moses another miracle in verses 6-7 and promised a third sign in verses 8-9, yet Moses gave God one last excuse in verse 10, when he claimed to be "slow of speech and tongue." Bible scholars have different views regarding whether or not Moses had an actual speech impediment or just an aversion to public speaking. Regardless, God was not swayed by his excuses.

READ EXODUS 4:11-12

Once again God countered Moses' objections with a revelation of Himself. He reminded Moses He was the one who created his mouth and gave him ability to speak. Did Moses really think God was going to say, "Oh, I did not realize that about you. Never mind, I will choose someone else"? How often do we present such excuses to God as if we think He has not thought His plan through completely? God is omniscient and knows more about us than we know about ourselves. When

He calls us to do something, it is with His full knowledge of whom He is calling.

Finally, in verse 13 Moses lays it on the line: he just did not want to go back to Egypt to face Pharaoh. That caused God's anger to burn as He recognized Moses' attitude as one of disobedience. He was finished listening to Moses' excuses and countered his apprehensions with promises of His equipping and power (see verses 15-16). Moses finally obeyed and went on to be the deliverer God called him to be.

God's power changed ordinary Moses into His powerful instrument for the deliverance of a nation. He changed an ordinary bush, dirt, and staff into holy miracles and an ordinary day into the beginning of a great mission.

Will you obey God's call and see what He can do with your "ordinary"? He may not be calling you to Egypt. He may be calling you to serve at church or to witness to that co-worker or neighbor. He may be calling you to surrender a part of your life you have been clinging to or to restore a broken relationship. He may be calling you to do something that is hard, but when you step out in obedience with an "even though" attitude, you will experience God's miraculous, sufficient, equipping power.

APPLICATION QUESTIONS

1. What are some things God did to get Moses' attention?

    What are some things He uses to get our attention today?

    Do you expect God to reveal Himself to you when you study His Word?

2. What excuses did Moses give to God?

    What are some excuses we give God when He calls us to do something difficult?

3. What promises did God give to Moses?

How do these promises encourage you?

4. Can you think of a time when you now see that God was working in a situation, even though you were not aware of it at the time?

   How can you be encouraged by this realization?

5. What attributes of God do you see in Exodus 3:1-4:17?

Thought for prayer this week
God equips those He calls.

In what areas do you need to stop making excuses to God? Ask Him for confidence in His equipping as you step out in obedience to Him.

GOING DEEPER

Look up these "I AM" statement made by Jesus and write down key words or phrases from each and what they mean to you:

John 6:35

John 8:12

John 10:9-10

John 10:11

John 11:25-26

John 14:6

John 15:1-5

Where are you trying to accomplish things for God in your own power?

Using your Bible's concordance or a Bible search, look up verses about OBEDIENCE.

Write down one or two promises tied to obedience.

Looking at these verses or this week's lesson, do you see one attribute of I AM that you particularly need to trust in with an "even though" attitude instead of a "yeah but" attitude?

What difference do you think focusing on that attribute will make in your daily life?

CHAPTER SIX
God's Power is Unlimited

Daniel 1-3: Daniel, Shadrach, Meshach and Abednego
When God says, "Nothing is impossible for me."

My sister recently recalled a time in the 1970's when she heard some adults arguing over whether or not Neil Armstrong had actually walked on the moon. Some folks thought the moon walk was completely staged in a production studio because space travel was impossible. When I was growing up the ultimate technology was having a phone cord long enough that you could step out of the kitchen and keep talking on the phone, hoping you were out of earshot of your mother. A phone that worked without a cord was impossible, never entering my mind. One computer took up an entire room because it was not possible for something smaller to have the same capabilities, or so we thought.

These things seemed impossible at the time, yet they are now not only possible but common-

> *Just because something has not happened yet does not mean it can't happen.*

place. They were not actually impossible; they just had not happened yet. The same is true when we are facing seemingly impossible situations in our lives.

In fact, God has promised that nothing is impossible for Him.

Daniel, Shadrach, Meshach and Abednego show how God did the impossible.

In the first 7 verses of Daniel 1, King Nebuchadnezzar, king of Babylon, besieged Jerusalem. God gave Nebuchadnezzar the victory over the Hebrews as foretold by His prophets (Isaiah 39, Micah 4:10). The Hebrews were exiled and the king took into Babylon the best of the best of the Hebrew youth to be trained for three years in preparation for service in his court. Daniel, Shadrach, Meshach, and Abednego were among those young men.

The purpose of the king's training was to transform these bright young men from Hebrews to Babylonians, teaching them a new language, culture, customs, ideas, and theology. They were given new names that glorified the Babylonian pagan gods rather than God Almighty. They were to eat the food from the king's table which would have been considered the best food available. However, that food and wine had likely been offered as sacrifices to their pagan gods and would not follow the dietary restrictions given to the Hebrews in the Law; therefore, it would defile them before God to partake of it.

READ DANIEL 1:8-14

Daniel and his friends resolved not to give in to external pressure, but to fully trust in God's equipping and sustaining power within them. That decision would bring glory to God in a pagan land. Instead of saying "Yeah, but we may face serious consequences if we refuse to do what they say in order to follow God's commands," they had the attitude of "We resolve to stay true to God's teaching even though we may face consequences as a result." This test of their resolve proved valuable to them in the future when they faced even greater tests.

Romans 12:2 states: *Do not conform to the pattern of this world, but be transformed by the renewing of your mind.*

The external pressures we face can tempt us to conform to the world's ways, but the power of God in us helps us successfully stand up to that pressure. Instead of being conformers and giving in to peer pressure, with God's power we learn to be transformers whose reliance on God glorifies Him and becomes an example to others.

> *God can do more with less than we can ever do on our own.*

God honored their resolve. After 10 days on a strict water and vegetable diet, they looked healthier and were better nourished than the others who had eaten the royal food.

God did more with water and vegetables than the others could do with a royal feast!

In verse 17 we see that God gave these young men knowledge and understanding as they trained. To Daniel, He gave a special ability to interpret dreams and visions. After three years of training, the king interviewed them and found that no one had knowledge and ability that was even close to theirs (verses 18-20).

READ DANIEL 2:1-3

King Nebuchadnezzar had a recurring nightmare that kept him from getting a good night's sleep. He called in his staff of magicians, enchanters, sorcerers, and astrologers to try to get an interpretation of the dream hoping he could find peace in knowing what it meant. Wisely, he tested them by insisting they first tell him what the dream was about. Of course, not one of them was able to do that.

READ DANIEL 2:10-11

The astrologers were forced to admit that what the king was asking was impossible for any man. What a blow to the reputation of fortune-tellers and astrologers. The contrast between the powerless Babylonian gods and the all-powerful One True God could not be any clearer. Acknowledging the source of the power to interpret the king's dream is crucial.

Their failure to interpret his dream made the king so angry he ordered the execution of all the wise men of Babylon, including Daniel and his friends, who apparently were not among those called in by the king. When Daniel heard about this order, he asked the king for more time so he could interpret the dream for him. Asking for this favor was risky for Daniel but his doing so exhibits that he had established a reputation of trustworthiness in the palace and that he had faith that God would provide the answer.

READ DANIEL 2:17-23

Daniel's example of how to approach a seemingly impossible situation with prayer offers several things we can apply (from verses 17-19).

Pray with friends.

Acknowledge your need for God's mercy.

Pray specifically.

Praise God.

Daniel praised God immediately when God revealed the mystery to him. He did not wait until he had gone before the king to see if what God had told him was correct. He praised God with confidence and trust, giving Him the glory.

READ DANIEL 2:26-28

Daniel went before the king to give him the interpretation he had asked for. When King Nebuchadnezzar asked if he could tell him his dream Daniel (like Joseph in Genesis 41:16) told him it was impossible for any man to do that.

> *The more impossible our situation seems, the greater the opportunity we have to experience God's possibilities.*

Verse 28 begins with a most important word: **But**. This is a powerful word in Scripture. "But God" is a gamechanging phrase indicating God's intervention in our hopeless situation. Daniel said it is impossible for man to do what the king asked, but God could reveal the mystery. The fact that it was impossible for man did not in any way limit God's ability and power.

Daniel gave King Nebuchadnezzar the answers he had been seeking. As he told the king what the dream meant he emphasized over and over that this was a message from God (verses 28, 29, 37, 44, 45). Daniel's answers led to the king acknowledging the One True God.

READ DANIEL 2:47-49

Daniel and others as well were personally blessed by his trust and obedience to God. More importantly, God was glorified as He accomplished the impossible. Even the Babylonian king's thinking was transformed when he witnessed the power of God.

However, in Chapter 3 King Nebuchadnezzar's pride and ego grew more than his spiritual insight. He had a giant image made of gold and set it up for everyone to see. He summoned all the officials to come to the dedication of the statue, and in verse 6 he declared that everyone (including the God-worshipping Jews) was required to bow down and worship it. The penalty for refusing to worship the image was death by way of being thrown into a blazing furnace.

READ DANIEL 3:8-12

These astrologers were probably alive thanks to Daniel and his friends halting their execution in chapter 2, but they had been shamed when God used Daniel to deliver the interpretation they were unable to discern. They were likely envious of the promotions Daniel and his friends received from the king. We do not know how much time had passed between chapters 2 and 3, but apparently, these astrologers had used that time to nurse their grudge against these God-fearing men. They went to King Nebuchadnezzar to tell him that Shadrach, Meshach, and Abednego were not complying with his order to worship the image.

The king was furious with rage and called in the three young men. In verses 14 and 15, as he was questioning them, he sounded incredulous: *Is it true that you do not serve my gods or worship the image I have set up?* He even offered them a second chance. He made sure they knew the conse-quences if they continued to refuse to worship the image: *If you do not worship it, you will be thrown immediately into a blazing furnace.* Then with his final question in verse 15, he demonstrated that he thought himself to be more powerful than any god, including their God when he asked, *Then what god will be able to rescue you from my hand?*

READ DANIEL 3:16-18

Shadrach, Meshach, and Abednego did not hesitate, argue with the king, or come up with excuses or compromises. They could have decided to bow down but not actually worship, or they could have justified giving in by saying they did it out of fear for their lives. They could have used rationalizations such as "God will understand." or "Everyone else is doing it." But they did none of those things. They had resolved to follow God. At all cost.

> *True faith is being obedient in spite of consequences.*

Remember that the power that enabled these young men to stand up to the external pressure came from God being with them, inside them, strengthening them. The external pressure from the world cannot stand up to the internal power of God when we resolve to be transformers, not conformers. This power in them was supernatural. It was divine. It was miraculous.

These three Hebrew men chose to put their faith in the One True God, the One who promised in Isaiah 43:1-3:

Do not fear, for I have redeemed you; I have summoned you by name; you are mine. When you pass through the waters, I will be with you; and when you pass through the rivers, they will not sweep over you. When you walk through the fire, you will not be burned; the flames will not set you ablaze. For I am the Lord your God, the Holy One of Israel, your Savior.

They did not know if God would literally fulfill that promise by keeping the flames from setting them ablaze or if He would allow them to be burned physically, but they knew either way God would rescue them from the king's hand (verse 17). The king could kill their bodies, but beyond that they were out of his reach. Because of their faith, their eternal destiny had already been determined. With the assurance of going to heaven, even physical death would have been deliverance from this world into Paradise. Nothing the king did could prevent that.

Note

Well-meaning people often misquote 1 Corinthians 10:13 claiming that it promises "God will never give you more than you can bear." That is not what that verse says and, in fact, that promise is not found anywhere in Scripture. In 2 Corinthians 1:8, Paul claimed they had been *"under great pressure, far beyond our ability to endure, so that we despaired even of life"* (emphasis mine). The 1 Corinthians verse is promising God will not allow you to be tempted beyond what you can bear, and that He will always provide you a way to stand up to the temptation. The truth is, God does allow circumstances into our lives that we cannot bear. Watching your child battling cancer, facing a terminal illness, seeing relationships and dreams fall apart can be unbearable. But God's promise to us is that we will never have

> to bear them alone (Isaiah 41:10, Deuteronomy 31:6, Joshua 1:9). There is nothing He can't handle. Shadrach, Meshach and Abednego were able to stay strong in an unbearable situation because of God's presence and power in their lives.

God will always deliver His children. Sometimes from death and sometimes through death, but He never fails to deliver them. Read verses 17 and 18 again: *We know the God we serve is able to save us from it...but even if He does not, we want you to know O king, that we will not serve your gods!* What a great "even though" attitude!

When He promises His presence, God is also promising His power.

How often is your praise and dedication to God dependent on getting your own way? If you are telling God "I will give you all the glory if only you will grant me what I am asking for" you are not trusting God...you are trying to make a deal with Him. Satan says, "If you worship me I will give you all this" (Matthew 4:9). God says, "Worship me because I am worthy to be worshipped" (2 Samuel 7:22).

Shadrach, Meshach and Abednego were saying, "We know God can do it. We don't have to know what God is going to do. We are going to praise Him and obey Him no matter what."

This response made the king angrier than ever. He had the furnace heated seven times hotter than usual, apparently trying to be sure survival would be impossible. He had them tied up and taken up to the furnace where the flames were so hot they killed the soldiers who were next to them.

READ DANIEL 3:24-25

God does not promise to always take you out of the fire, but He does promise to always be with you in it.

When Nebuchadnezzar looked into the fire, he saw not three men but four. The fourth man in the fire was God Himself, the pre-incarnate Christ. Remember from our past lessons how powerful it is when God promises to be with us.

There is no fire we face that God can't put out, but sometimes His sovereign plan calls for allowing it to burn. Rather than feeling frustrated when God allows the fire in your life, trust that He is with you and know that He is allowing it for a reason.

READ DANIEL 3:26-27

The only things burned by the fire were the ropes that had bound the men. Don't lose sight of the fact that the harder King Nebuchadnezzar tried to make their deliverance impossible, the greater God's glory was when He accomplished it.

In verses 28-29 King Nebuchadnezzar recognized the power of God that delivered Shadrach, Meshach, and Abednego. He praised Him and declared that no one was to say anything against their God. In another example of how God can use even pagan kings to accomplish His plan, everyone who gathered for the dedication of the image was then witness to the power of Almighty God.

The difference between these three young Hebrew men and everyone else who was gathered was not the *presence* of faith, because everyone has faith in something. The difference was the *object* of their faith. Putting faith in something that is not true and trustworthy leads to disappointment and ultimately to death. But when you put your faith in El Shaddai, which means "Almighty God for whom nothing is impossible", you will find life, hope, freedom, and deliverance.

> No matter how God answers, He is still God and worthy of praise and obedience.

When you start to feel like your situation is impossible remember God promises that nothing is impossible for Him and you can take Him at His word.

APPLICATION QUESTIONS

1. What things did Daniel, Shadrach, Meshach and Abednego resolve not to do?

   Why was it important to them to not do these things?

   What are some things the world offers that we, as followers of Christ, need to resolve to avoid?

2. How can your resolve to be a "transformer" instead of a "conformer" affect others?

3. Can you recall a time when God has done the impossible for you?

As you wait for God to act, how is your attitude affected when you trust that nothing is impossible for God?

4. Why do you think God does not always intervene to stop our suffering?

5. What do you find significant about these facts in Daniel 3:
   o The flames were so hot the soldiers standing nearby were killed. (v 22)
   o The three men were firmly tied up. (v 23)
   o Nothing on them was scorched or even smelled like fire. (v 28)
   o The king declared "No other god can save in this way." (v 29)

6. What attributes of God do you see in Daniel
   1-3?

Thought for prayer this week
In *Luke 18:27 Jesus replied, "What is impossible
with men is possible with God."*

Ask God to show you where you need to trust
Him even though your situation feels impossible.

GOING DEEPER

How do these verses relate to this week's lesson? How do they relate to you?

Exodus 20:3

Psalm 50:15

Jeremiah 32:27

Hebrews 11:25- 27

1 Peter 1:7

Romans 8:31

Read Daniel's prayer in Daniel 2:20-23. Write it in your own words then pray it back to God as a prayer of praise and thanksgiving.

CONCLUSION

Review the lessons from this study. As you look over them, use these questions to recall and apply the things you have learned.

1. Which of these promises has encouraged you most since you began this study?

   How has it encouraged you?

2. In what situations have you been able to change your "yeah, but" attitude to one of "even though"?

   What was the result?

3. Have you shared with anyone else the things you have learned during this study? What did you share?

4. What did you learn about God that you did not know before?

5. What did you learn about yourself?

6. Do you have a favorite verse that you discovered while studying the promises of God?

7. What attribute of God has meant the most to you during this study?

8. How have you seen God answer your prayers as you have trusted in His promises?

The promises in this study are just the beginning. Scripture is full of promises from God to His children. As you have studied these promises from God and have seen them in action in the lives of Abraham, Moses, Joseph, Daniel and his friends, I hope you have been able to become intentional about your "even though" attitude.

You may find starting a journal helpful as you read and study the Bible. Every time you read a promise of God write it down then meditate on it and ask God to help you apply it to your life. Once you begin to take God at His word, you can replace your "yeah, but" attitude with one of "even though." Then you will experience the life change that comes with trust in God Almighty.

FROM THE AUTHOR

I hope you enjoyed your study of God's promises and found this book to be a helpful resource. I pray that God will richly bless you as you seek to know Him better. It is my hope that you will find joy in experiencing God's faithfulness as His promises become more and more real to you.

If you would like to contact me for any reason, you can reach me through my email address: info@eventhough.net. I would enjoy hearing from you.

Julie McCoy

More Books from Greentree Publishers

For more information on these and other titles, visit our website at greentreepublishers.com

Immovable: Standing Firm in the Last Days

By Tim Riordan

Does Bible prophecy indicate that we are living in the last days? What should Christians do to be ready for the days ahead? Dr. Tim Riordan shares biblical truths on Bible prophecy and how the Church can stand firm in the last days.

Songs from the Heart: Meeting with God in the Psalms

By Tim Riordan

You will enjoy this Bible study/devotional on one of the most loved books of the Bible: the Psalms. Join Dr. Tim Riordan as he shares insights on these beloved passages through Bible teaching and storytelling, making personal application to your life.

Made in the USA
Columbia, SC
23 August 2019